Peggy Ratliff Ministries

1001 Central Ave.
Metairie, LA 70001

Peggy Ratliff Ministries trade paperback edition
June 2014.
Unless otherwise noted, all Scripture quotations are from
the New King James Version of the Bible

For more information about bulk purchases, speaking
engagements, and signings, please contact Pastor Peggy
Ratliff at 1-866-940-3339 or
peggyratliffministries@gmail.com
www.pastorpeggy.org

Designed & Edited by Adonis White-Price
thebusinesspro7@gmail.com

Manufactured in the United States of America
ISBN: 978-0-9961294-1-1

Contents

This Prayer book is dedicated to my deceased grandmother
Rosetta Bourgeois Morris,
my foundation in prayer started with her.

May my six Grandchildren's prayer life
be stronger because of this work...

This book is also dedicated to all the members of Holy
Trinity Outreach Ministry, where prayer is our foundation.

Pastor Peggy Ratliff

Acknowledgements

Thank you to our Heavenly Father for trusting me with his word and giving me his wisdom to do this work.

I wish to express my deepest appreciation to my husband Benton Ratliff, for his constant support and encouragement, for giving me the time to do this work for the Kingdom. This word was birthed during the late hours of the night.

To my spiritual daughter Pastor Sandra Ellis, who worked on this project with me in the beginning stages of getting people to pray. You were then, and still stand, as a prayer partner to this day. To my spiritual daughter Pastor Laura Price, thank you for your love, prayers, support, and always being there.

To Minister Adonis Price, who immediately saw the vision and came on board to make this handbook a reality, your creativity and attention to detail are a blessing to me. To Elder Gardenia Crockett, for her insight adding the title to this work. To our church administrator Pamela Harris, who lifts the everyday load off that I may be more productive.

To my dear mother Celestine Dunbar, for always being there and praying me through, teaching me to never quit and always trust God. To my beautiful daughters Keishia Henderson and Alicia Skinner, for sharing me with the world, I pray that I am an example that you would be proud to follow.

To all of my partners & friends, for their support and prayers.

I Love you all…

INTRODUCTION

Before you get started, ask yourself what is it that you want to accomplish by investing your time in this manual? Do you know if you are connected with God in prayer?

I had been in church all my life but I was still a baby in many areas of my life, primarily prayer. Since I hadn't grown in my prayer life, it was difficult to grow in any other area of my spiritual walk with God.

I needed a mediator (a middle man) to talk to the Lord for me. I had not developed a personal relationship with our Heavenly Father for myself. I wanted to be used by God, I wanted to be anointed, but I was not doing enough to increase my knowledge about Him.

One day many years ago, I heard a sermon preached titled "Who's in control of your prayer life? What if they decide to stop praying for you, then what?" That hit home for me. I was depending on everyone else to pray for me, and it was time that I learn how to pray for myself.

What I discovered was there were some things about me that my God would not share with anyone else, but me. It was in my private time with God that he began to reveal His perfect plan for my life. Revelation comes through relationship, relationship comes through prayer…

Now…that's a little bit of my story, so let's get back to my question to you; what is it that you need the Lord to do for you spiritually? Once you know the answer to that question then you are ready to begin your study of this handbook.

"Simple Instructions of Prayer" (SIP) was created about three years ago. I found myself spending a great amount of time in counseling with people that weren't sure if they were praying correctly or even if God was hearing their prayers. What I found was there were a lot of questions about prayer. I would recommend a prayer manual to them, but for some reason they came back with even more questions. With so many great manuals and prayer books out there I did not see the need for another one.

Originally this was written for in-house Bible study on "simple instructions of prayer" (SIP). What started out as a Bible study became the tool that made praying clearer. In this prayer book, I simply deal with the most asked questions. What I've discovered is that not only babes in Christ have difficulty with prayer. Some who have been sitting in church all their lives have questions about if God hears them.If someone is constantly needing someone else to pray for them in every situation, this person is struggling with their prayer life. I pray that this prayer handbook will bring the reader into a greater relationship and communicating with our Heavenly Father.

Psalm 16:11 tells us *"you will make known to me the path of life; in your presence is fullness of joy; in your right hand there are pleasures forever."* NAS

I look forward to hearing your testimony…

Pastor Peggy Ratliff

Chapter 1

WHAT IS PRAYER

Prayer is *(talking)* between God and people. The word *pray* means ' tell me'. *Supplication* is to 'make a humble request or petition earnestly'. There is communication taking place, the act of transmitting your call and receiving God's answer. The telephone is one way of transmitting talking between two parties; likewise, prayer transmits our heart to God. In prayer, we commune with God. The word *commune* means to ' share, talk intimately, administer or make a deposit'. You are giving something to God and God is imparting something into you.

Prayer
Pre(ə)r/
A solemn request for help or expression of thanks addresses to God
~

THE FIRST TIME

At first it may seem hard to share your heart with God.
You don't know enough about Him, so you feel funny or
strange talking to God...someone you cannot see.
Let's look at Moses in Exodus 3:6, Moses was afraid the
first time he has to talk to the Lord, so afraid that he hid
his face. The more he did it (talk to the Lord), you will
find that in Exodus 33:11 that *the Lord spoke to Moses
face to face, as a man speaks to his friend.*" Moses went from
hiding his face to being friendly. The word *friendly*
means 'easily used or understood by'. It was difficult
for Moses at first, but as he understood communication
through prayer it became easy.

GET TO KNOW THE SPIRIT OF GOD WITHIN

1 Corinthians 3:16 says *"Do you not know that you are the
temple of God and that the Spirit of God dwells in you?"*

John 4:24 tells us that *"God is spirit"* so the natural eye does not see him. God created us in His image, that means you are body, spirit, and soul (mind). The Lord created us that way so we can talk and pray to Him in our spirit. Just like the Lord, the natural eye can not see our spirit, but we all have one, and to our surprise it is the spirit of God that lives on the inside of us. When you believed in the Lord Jesus and are baptized, it is then that you need the Spirit of God to communicate though the Spirit. Look at Acts 19:1-6, The Apostle Paul talks to some of the disciples at Corinth and he asks them, did they received the Holy Spirit since they believed? Their response was, *"we have not so much as heard whether there be any Holy Spirit."* Just like those disciples, there was a time when I had not heard of the precious Holy Spirit. The disciples were

Just like the Lord The natural eye cannot see our spirit, but we all have one, and to our surprise it is the spirit of God that lives on the inside of us. ~

baptized and believed on the Lord Jesus Christ, but they were not filled with the Holy Spirit.

It is through the Holy Spirit that you will be able to resist the devil.

~

That might be you! The good news is, after the Apostle Paul taught them they received the word of the Lord and were filled with the Holy Spirit. My prayer for you is that if you have not yet received the gift of the Holy Spirit, after this teaching you will receive the Holy Spirit.

The Spirit of God is so important to your prayer life. John 16:13 says *"when the spirit of truth comes, he will guide you into all truth."*

In Ezekiel 36:26-27 the Lord says *"I will give you a new heart and put a new spirit in you; I will remove from you your heart of stone and give you a heart of flesh. I will put my Spirit within you and cause you to walk in my ways."* If you have not already experienced the Holy Spirit operating in your life, spend some time studying the

Scriptures on the Holy Spirit. It is through the Holy Spirit that you will be able to resist the devil.

Acts 1:8 tells us *"you will receive power after that the Holy Spirit has come upon you."*

1 Corinthians 3:16 says *"do you not know that you are the temple of God and that the Spirit of God dwells in you?"*

Let that soak in. Say with me: the spirit of the Lord lives in me. Close your eyes and say: the spirit of the Lord lives in me.

Colossians 3:16 says *"tell us to let the word of Christ dwell in you richly, in all wisdom."*

The more you know about the Holy Spirit and the word of God, the greater your communication with your Heavenly Father will be. When you learn to pray the word, you are communicating to God you know who he is and what he can do.

The Bible tells us in Romans 8:26, *"the Holy Spirit helps us in our weakness. We do not know what we ought to pray for, but the Spirit himself intercedes for us through groans."*

Ephesians 3:20 is a Scripture we like to quote, *"now unto him that is able to do exceeding abundantly above all that we ask or think."* And that's where we stop reading. We thank the Lord that He's going to do exceeding and abundantly in our lives, then in our spirit; we are waiting on God.

Now read the rest of that Scripture, *"according to the power that worketh in us."* Where does the power have to be? Yes, in you! The power is the Holy Spirit of God. You are not waiting on God. He is waiting on you to receive the Holy Spirit. According to Acts 1:8, *"you will receive power after that the Holy Spirit has come upon you."*

I cannot stress this enough! Getting to know the Spirit of God within you is essential to your walk with the Lord.

WE HAVE TO BE TAUGHT TO PRAY

The disciples also needed help with prayer. The disciple said 'teach us to pray', this is an indication that we have to be taught to pray.

Luke 11:1-4 says *"and it came to pass, that, as he was praying in a certain place, when he ceased, one of his disciples said unto him, 'Lord, teach us to pray, as John also taught his disciples.' And He said unto them 'When ye pray say: Our Father which art in heaven, hallowed be thy name. Thy kingdom come. Thy will be done, as in heaven, so in earth. Give us day by day our daily bread. And forgive us our sins; for we also forgive every one that is indebted to us. And lead us not into temptation; but deliver us from evil'."*

Jesus was giving them an example of all their needs

being met in praying to our Heavenly Father. You have to start seeing God as your Father. In the natural, you have your father's DNA as proof that you are his child. In the spirit, your DNA is the Spirit of God that is your proof.

The first three parts of prayer represent the will of God.

The First: "Thy kingdom come."

The Second: "Thy will be done."

The Third: "In heaven and in earth."

The scripture declares in Philippians 4:19, *"God shall supply all your needs, but His will must come first."*

The last three parts of prayer represent God supplying all the needs of His people.

The First: Our daily bread.

The Second: Forgiveness.

The Third: Guidance.

So you see, you don't need a lot of words, just make sure your words are not empty. Empty words are full of pride, arrogance, and selfishness.

Matthew 6:7-8 tells us *"when you pray, don't babble on and on as people of other religions do. They think their prayers are answered merely by repeating their word s again and again. Don't be like them, for your Father knows exactly what you need even before you ask him."*

Listen to the dialogue that Jesus, the master teacher, uses: *Our Father, give us this day our daily bread, forgive us our debts, as we forgive.* The words he used, *we* and *our*, they protect us and unite us.

Chapter 2

LEARN THE PRINCIPLES OF GOD

Hebrews 11:6 says *"but without faith it is impossible to please him: for he that comes to God must believe that he is, and that he is a rewarder of them that diligently seek him."*

Hebrews 11:6 tells us three things that are important when you pray.

1st. YOU NEED FAITH TO PLEASE GOD

What is faith? Most definitions say that *faith* is 'belief' or 'trust'. I believe that this is exactly what our Heavenly Father wants us to have; trust in Him. For the word says in Hebrews 11:6, *"for he that comes to God must believe that he is.*

Without Faith it is impossible to please God.
~

" That he is what? Able. You see that word MUST. He is saying either you do believe God and trust Him, or you don't. There is no maybe, you must have confidence in what you believe. You may be asking, "Why is it so important?" The word tells us that it is impossible to please God without faith. What you will need faith for, is to believe in God for something that, without his help, cannot happen.

This where it gets a little tricky. The more you pray, the more it will appear as if the situation is getting worse. You may ask, "Why?" It's because Satan wants you to doubt God and believe that God can't do what you need. You make the devil a liar and please God when you don't believe the lie that Satan is trying to tell you.

The more you pray the more it will appear as if the situation is getting worse.

~

Remember the story of Jairus in Mark 5, whose daughter was at the point of death, and he prayed to Jesus and asked Him to come and *"lay thy hands on her, that she may be healed."* But before Jesus could get to the house, someone came and said to Jairus *"thy daughter is dead."* Remember, I told you it gets tricky! Look at what Jesus says in Mark 5:36 — *"Don't be afraid, only believe."* I'm going to paraphrase it for you, Jesus was saying to Jairus 'don't be afraid, only believe what you prayed for'. We have to do the same thing, only believe the word of God.

2nd. BELIVE THAT HE IS GOD

The word will remind you of who God is in difficult times. The Bible tells us in Psalm 103:7 that *"He made known his ways to Moses, his acts or deeds to the people of Israel."*

What is the difference between Moses and the children of Israel? The children of Israel knew the acts or the miracles that God performed on their behalf, and they didn't develop a relationship with God. They were just concerned about getting what they wanted.

Do you know people who only call you when they want something? Just like people today, the children of Israel soon forgot what God had done for them, and *"forgot his works, and his wonders that he had shown them,"* (Psalm 78:11).

In Exodus 33:13 Moses wanted more, so he prayed this prayer: *"If you are pleased with me, teach me your ways so I may know you and continue to find favor with you."*

We can never please God if we don't know him. Moses was looking for a relationship. This is what God said about Himself in Isaiah 55:8-9, *"My thoughts are not your thoughts, neither are your ways my ways. For as the heavens are higher than the earth, so are my ways higher than your ways, and my thoughts than your thoughts."* Just as Moses prayed, we must pray the same prayer so our Heavenly Father can reveal Himself to us, as he did to Moses.

3rd. SINCERELY SEEK HIM

Seek means 'to go in search or quest of: to try to find or discover by searching or questioning: to try to obtain'.

You seek God by searching out the Scriptures to obtain revelation through the Holy Spirit. Our third point says to 'sincerely seek', the meaning of this is in Deuteronomy 4:29, *"seek the Lord thy God, and you will find Him if you search for Him with all your Heart and all your soul."*

When you sincerely seek the Lord, it says you trust him for the answer and for him to show you the way. Your Heavenly Father will be pleased with you when you seek Him and trust Him and only Him.

Matthew 6:33 tells us to *"seek first the kingdom of God, and His righteousness,"* and then you can get the things you want, but God is first!

I know you have heard the saying 'God first, family next', but what does it really mean to put God first? Think for a moment about what is first in your life, be honest. There was a time in my life that I loved God but I loved myself more. I was more concerned about what I wanted rather than what the Lord required. I was not committed to my church or my obligations, but I wanted God to be committed to me. When I needed something, I wanted the Lord to meet that need, even if I wasn't committed.

When I heard the scripture Galatians 6:7, "*be not deceived; God is not mocked; for whatsoever a man sows, that shall he also reap,*" I said 'Amen' to it, not really knowing what that meant. But to my surprise, I was getting ready to find out. The only time I would

I wanted the Lord to meet my needs, even if I wasn't committed.
~

pray was when I wanted something. Because when I wanted something from my mom, I would be very loving and it would get me what I wanted. I did the same thing to the Lord. Then I would hear this Scripture, *"God is not mocked."* This was all the Lord would say to me. I had no gratitude. I assumed, just as I did with my mom, that God had to do it because he was obligated to do it. I got tired of that answer, and I asked the Lord one day, "What are you saying?" and this is what the Lord said to me. It changed my life. I pray that it changes yours too.

The Lord said, "I am only obligated to those who put me first." After that, I became committed to praying and seeking the Lord's help in how to put Him first. What I learned was, by being obligated to my church and the things of God, I was putting God first.

We should always pray the will of God in all situations.

God is all knowing and has a perfect plan for every situation.

~

He is all knowing and has a perfect plan for the situations that arise in our lives. Our Heavenly Father wants the true goodness of heaven to be revealed in the earth through our lives.

OBEDIENCE

Obedience is the act or practice of 'obeying, being dutiful, submissive, or in compliance with someone in command' (God).

In Isaiah 1:19 the scripture explains to us *"if we are willing and are obedient, you shall eat the good of the land."* Through prayer we gain the ability to hear the voice of God. When we obey what God tells us to do, we put ourselves in alignment to be blessed by God.

In your private reading time, look at what God has to say about obedience in Deuteronomy 28.

MEDITATE

To *meditate* is the practice of 'turning your attention to a single point of reference'. It means to focus on one thing at that present moment and turn your attention away from things that may come to distract or prevent you from what you're focusing on.

In Joshua 1:8 the scripture tells us to *"meditate on the word of God day and night, then you will make your way prosperous, and then you shall have good success."* Could it be that easy? Yes, when you learn the principles. When you learn these principles, your confidence in your prayer life will shift.

LEARN TO USE THE KEYS

In Matthew 16:19, Jesus said *"I will give you the keys of the kingdom of heaven."* In the last part of the verse a very important key is given: binding and loosing— *"whatever you bind on earth will be bound in heaven, and whatever you loose on earth will be loosed in heaven."* The keys to the kingdom will open doors that no man can close, and close doors that no man can open. You have the keys, so you can permit a thing, or not permit it. The choice is yours. Learn to use the keys. For example: if sickness is giving you trouble, bind up the spirit of infirmity (sickness) and loose the supernatural healing virtue of God.

Prayer is when you go to God, our Heavenly Father, humbly and earnestly, not with vain repetitions but with your sincere desires, petitions, or requests.

Matthew 6:5-6 says *"when you pray, don't be like the hypocrites who love to pray publicly on street corners and in the synagogues where everyone can see them. I tell you the truth, that is all the reward they will ever get." "But when you pray, go away by yourself, shut the door behind you, and pray to your Father in private. Then your Father, who sees everything, will reward you."*

Chapter 3

JESUS KNOWS ALL ABOUT FORGIVENESS

In Matthew 6:14-15 it says *"if you forgive those who sin against you, your Heavenly Father will forgive you. But if you refuse to forgive others, your Father will not forgive your sins."*

Your heart has to be right. Forgiveness is part of getting your prayers answered. God forgives us, and

Forgiveness is a part of getting your prayers answered.
~

we have to forgive others. You may say, "You don't know what they did to me, how they hurt me, I can't forgive them." I agree with you, you can't forgive on your own. Pray to the Father earnestly and sincerely about forgiveness.

What is prayer? It is coming clean with God about your hurts, disappointments, fears, anger, weaknesses, and whatever questions you may have. Remember, Jesus knows all about forgiveness and how important it is to forgive quietly. When Jesus was still on the cross in the midst of his pain and agony, He said in Luke 23:34, *"Father forgive them, for they know not what they do."* Jesus understood that all things work together for our good.

It may appear as though Jesus lost the battle at Calvary, but let's take a look. The one he called 'friend' betrayed Him. The one who said he would never leave Him and would die for Him was cursing, swearing, and denying he ever knew Jesus. The other disciples scattered, but Jesus was victorious because he was able to forgive, and you can too.

If you have difficulty forgiving someone, say this prayer with me: *Father God, help me to release this person and forgive them. I can't do this alone. I need your help in Jesus' name!*

Do this as often as needed. You will know when

forgiveness has taken place, there will be freedom and a release in your spirit.

Prayer is more than you asking for things such as houses, cars, or even healing. Matthew 6:25-34 says that your Heavenly Father is already aware that you need all these things. In prayer, you will receive so much more than things. He gives us Rest, Peace, and Love— for example—and so much more.

REST

Matthew 11:27-28 tells us *"then Jesus said, 'Come to me, all of you who are weary and carry heavy burdens, and I will give you rest'."*

PEACE

In John 14:27 Jesus says *"I am leaving you with a gift— peace of mind and heart. And the peace I give is a gift the world cannot give. So don't be troubled or afraid."*

LOVE

1 John 4:19 says *"we love him, because he first loved us."*

All the things you need you will find in prayer from God Almighty. God has worked and is working many miracles through genuine prayer. Jesus tells us in Luke 4:18 that he *"was sent to heal the brokenhearted."* I know you are thinking about the person or the people who hurt you or did you wrong; Jesus can help, will you let him heal you today?

A TIME OF REFLECTION

Before you move forward, take some time to reflect on what you have understood to this point. What has hit home for you? What changes have you made, or do you need to make, thus far? What is your goal by the end of this book?

_____

_____

_____

_____

_____

_____

_____

_____

_____

_____

_____

_____

_____

_____

Chapter 4

THE LIVING GOD

You must call on the name of God our Heavenly Father, the God of Abraham, Isaac, and Jacob. He is the only true and living God.

In 1 Kings 18:27, Elijah began to mock the prophets of Baal, saying *"cry louder to your god, perhaps he is sleeping."* There are many false gods, and Baal is just one of them. They are dead and cannot hear you when you call. Have you ever had someone come into your life that you thought came to be

You must call on the name of God, our Heavenly Father.
~

a blessing? They came saying what they were going to do and be in your life. When it was time to produce, they were nowhere to be found, or they were silent because they could not produce.

Jeremiah 33:3 says *"call unto me, and I will answer thee, and show thee great and mighty things, which thou knowest not."* Our Heavenly Father never sleeps nor slumbers, He will answer every time.

Chapter 5

WHY PRAY

Jesus was always praying. Prayer displays Jesus' unity with the Father. Jesus had morning devotion (Mark 1:35), evening prayer (Mark 6:46), and solitary prayer (Luke 5:16); Jesus prayed all night (Luke 6:12).

We can not operate in the power and authority of the Father God without prayer.
~

In times of trouble we are to cast our cares upon him in prayer (1 Peter 5:7). Jesus in the Garden of Gethsemane was casting his care on the Father (Luke 22:41-42). Prayer was priority with Jesus, and He is our example in prayer. Take a look at Luke 11:1—after Jesus finished praying, one of his disciples said, *"Lord, teach us to pray."* The disciples had walked with Jesus long enough to know that prayer was the key to who He was in the Spirit. Jesus could not operate in the power and authority of the Father, (God Almighty), without prayer. Wherever Jesus went, miracles, signs, and wonders followed Him. But there was a promise for us, (the believer), regarding the works of Jesus. He said, in John 14:12, *"Greater works shall you do, but you must ask the Father."* In other words, you must pray. In prayer, you will see the power of God in your life, just like it was in the life of Jesus. Prayer brings oneness with you and the Father; His will becomes your

In prayer you will see the power of God in your life just like it was in the life of Jesus.
~

will. Through prayer and studying God's word, we learn the Father's will. *(Thy will be done)*, God's will is that it may be done on earth as it is in heaven. In heaven there is nothing missing, nothing broken, nothing lacking; the same is what God wants for you in your life. We pray so God can do a work in our lives. We are being transformed through the renewing of our mind when we come to prayer. Romans 12:2 tells us that spiritual transformation starts in the mind and heart. In Psalm 51:10, David asked God to *"create in me a clean heart and renew the right spirit within me."* God is the only source of such a renewal; but the word *transformed* means to 'change from the old man to the new man'.

"Therefore if any man is in Christ he is a new creature, old things have passed away and behold, all things are become new," (2 Corinthians 5:17). In our prayer life, the old sinful ways will pass from us, and the new man, which is our new life in Jesus Christ, dying to sin and living for Christ. The old man is under an old master, (Satan); the new man has a new master living within, (the Spirit of God). I believe that many believers have not spent enough time in prayer for the change to take place. In order for the change from the old man to the new man to take place, you must spend quality time in prayer so that the Lord can do the work. You can spend time, but if it is not quality time it will not produce a new life for you—this is why prayer is so important. Half-hearted prayer will produce half-hearted change. The effectual, fervent prayers of the righteous availeth much. Jesus had a strong private secret prayer

life (Matthew 6:6). Find yourself a secret place and shut the door, because the Father wants to develop a relationship with you. In this secret place you will come to know that still small voice (1 Kings 19:12).

In John 10:4-5 Jesus says *"For my sheep know my voice, and a stranger they will not follow."* It is in the secret place that you come to know who you are in God, and He gives us dominion and blesses us.

We are a chosen generation, a royal priesthood, a holy nation, a peculiar people; know that you have been called out of darkness into His marvelous light (1 Peter 2:9). If you spend time in secret, God will reward you openly. It is in public that men will begin to see your good works and glorify your Father in heaven (Matthew 5:16).

Why pray? Because without it, you cannot commune with the Heavenly Father. The Word of God instructs us to pray without ceasing (1 Thessalonians 5:17). You must also watch in prayer, *"keep watch that you may not enter into temptation; because your spirit man is willing, but the flesh is weak,"* (Matthew 26:41). You are only as strong as your prayer life.

Now is the time to seek the Lord more than ever before. Prayer is God's birthing room. This is where miracles take place, in prayer. This is where you hear the heart of God. What does He have to say regarding your life? God wants to commune, converse, connect, and have intimacy — a face to face encounter with you. This happens only in prayer. Will you answer His call and enter in? He's waiting for you!

Chapter 6

THE CRY ~ THE CALL IN PRAYER

"And it came to pass in the process of time, that the king of Egypt died; and the children of Israel signed by reason of the bondage, and they cried, and their cry came up unto God by reason of the bondage. And God heard their groaning, and God remembered His covenant with Abraham, with Isaac, and with Jacob. And God looked upon the children of Israel, and God had respect unto them," (Exodus 2:23-25).

> **And God heard their groaning and God remembered His covenant with Abraham, with Isaac, and with Jacob. (Exodus 2:24) ~**

In Exodus 2:23-25, the children of Israel cried out to the Lord and the Bible says their cry came up to God. He heard it and moved in mercy and compassion on their behalf. God hears the cries of His people.

"Call unto me, and I will answer thee, and show thee great and mighty things, which thou knows not," (Jeremiah 33:3).

"The righteous cry and the LORD hears, and delivers them out of all their troubles," (Psalm 34:17).

"I cried unto the Lord with my voice, and He heard me from His holy hill," (Psalm 3:4).

"Hear me when I call, O God of my righteousness! You have relieved me in my distress; have mercy on me, and hear my prayer," (Psalm 4:1).

"Give ear to my words O Lord, consider my meditation. Hearken unto the voice of my cry, my King and my God; for unto thee will I pray. My voice shalt thou hear in the morning, OLORD; in the morning will I direct my prayer unto thee, and will look up," (Psalm 5:1-3).

David knew that God was his shield and a very present help in the time of trouble. There were times when

David had sinned, but because he had a repentant heart he found the mercy of God. He was restored and delivered. God showed up on David's behalf time and time again. He will do the same for you, but you must ask. The scriptures above represent David asking God multiple times.

Psalm 34:19 says it like this: *"many are the afflictions of the righteous; but the Lord delivers him out of them all."*

He will move heaven and earth on the behalf of the righteous. Not just in some of his afflictions, troubles, and times of despair, but out of them all shall we find deliverance.

Hallelujah to the Lamb of God!

Chapter 7

PRAISE IN PRAYER

"I will bless the LORD at all times, His praise shall continually be in my mouth," (Psalm 34:1). That does not mean 'just in good days'. The word *continually* means 'no matter what the situation, I will praise You because

And we know that all things work together for the good to them that love God. (Romans 8:28)

~

I know you as God Almighty, and all things are working together for my good'. Praise shows your level of trust in God.

You have seen, or should begin to see, the hand of God move on your behalf over and over again.

Praise comes from a Latin word meaning 'value' or 'price', to give praise to God is to proclaim His merit or worth. *Hallelujah* is Hebrew for 'praise the Lord'. It is also the highest praise we can honor God with. In times of trouble, we need to say "Hallelujah," — you have grown spiritually when you can praise the Lord in the midst of trouble. You may say, "That's easy for me to say", but let's take a look at one of our Patriarchs (Job).

"So Satan answered the Lord and said: does Job fear God for nothing? Have you not made a hedge around him, around his household, and around all that he has on every side? You have blessed the work of his hands, and his possessions have increased in the land. But now, stretch out Your hand and touch all that he has, and he will surely curse You to Your face," (Job 1:9-12).

The Bible says that Job was a very wealthy man and his wealth came from the Lord, but one day the Lord gave Satan permission to attack Job. Satan was not just out to take things

Though He slay me, yet will I trust him. (Job 13:15)
~

from Job—he knew that God would restore all these things to Job—it was his character Satan was after. The game plan of S a t a n is for you to curse or disrespect God, to lose faith and heart in God. Even though Job had one bad report after another, he did not sin against God. The testimony of Job was *"though He slay me, yet will I trust in Him,"* (Job 13:15). In all these things, Job did not sin or charge God with wrong. The Bible goes on to say he worshipped God and blessed His name (Job 1:20-21). Just as Job, your praise and your worship will give you the strength to bless the Name of the Lord. Praise should originate in the heart and should not be a mere outward show. *"This people draw nigh unto me with their mouth and honor me with their lips; but their heart is far from me,"* (Matthew 15:8). We must praise Him in Spirit and in Truth.

When in battle, I believe praise is the greatest weapon you can have. When you have some time, read 2 Chronicles 20. Jehoshaphat and the children of Israel were in the battle of their lives. In verse 21, it says *"Jehoshaphat appointed singers unto the Lord, that should praise the name of the Lord."* In verse 22, they *"began to sing and praise"* and the Bible says the Lord *"sent an ambush against their enemy."*

Read the story. You will find that the children of Israel were victorious because of their praise. When you are in the middle of a battle your praise will confuse the enemy. It worked for the children of Israel and it will work for you. Use your weapon of praise on that situation you're facing right now! The more you use your weapon of praise, the more effective it will become. Remember, Satan doesn't want you praising God, he wants you to praise him. Look what he tells Jesus in Matthew 4:9, *"Satan said unto Jesus: all these things will I give thee if thou wilt fall down and worship me."*

Let the praises of our God continually be in your mouth.

Chapter 8

WORSHIP IN PRAYER

Worship is different from praise in the sense that in praise we proclaim God's goodness, merit, or worth. But in worship, we honor God, we show forth our love to the Father for who He is to us and what He is doing through us. Our dance breaks forth in true worship.

Worship is different from praise

~

Worship says, " I have already seen and experienced your goodness and mercy; and that goodness is deserving of reward. That reward is my heartfelt praise." Our worship will take us places that praise cannot go!

"And it came to pass, when Moses went out unto the tabernacle, that all the people rose up and stood every man at his tent door and looked after Moses, until he was gone into the tabernacle. And it came to pass, as Moses entered into the tabernacle, the cloudy pillar descended and stood at the door of the tabernacle and the Lord talked to Moses. And

all the people saw the cloudy pillar stand at the tabernacle door, and the Lord spoke unto Moses face-to-face, as a man speaks unto his friend. And he turned again into the camp; but his servant Joshua the son of Nun, a young man, departed not out of the tabernacle," (Exodus 33:8-11).

The people of God watched as Moses went to worship the Lord. God does not want us to worship afar off. He wants us to come close so we can feel His presence and know His ways. The Lord spoke to Moses face-to-face, as a man speaks to a friend. The Lord desires to become your friend. Joshua wanted what Moses had, so he

God wants us to come close to him through Worship while in Prayer, so we can feel his presence.

did as he saw Moses do; he stayed and worshiped long after Moses was gone. From a distance, the people saw the pillar, recognized the presence of God, and they worshiped by bowing to the ground. What was the difference between the worship of Moses and the people? It was their communication. Moses wanted more than just to see God's presence, he wanted to experience His presence.

"Now therefore, I pray thee, if I have found grace in thy sight, show me now thy way, that I may know you, that I may find grace in thy sight," (Exodus 33:13). Moses said, "Show me who you really are. I have seen your signs and wonders. I know you can do anything. I have seen your mighty powers, but now I want to experience you in a greater way."

"He made known His ways unto Moses, His acts unto the children of Israel," (Psalm 103:7). Let us not follow in the ways of the children of Israel, only bowing in His presence and never asking for more of Him. *"This people draw near unto me with their mouth, and honor me with their lips, but their heart is far from me,"* (Matthew 15:8). What a concept. We cannot worship God without our hearts being in it. It is our heart that speaks to God.

"God is spirit, and his worshipers must worship in spirit and in truth," (John 4:24).

Chapter 9

HEART OF THANKSGIVING IN PRAYER

You will find that people who have a heart of thanksgiving understand that they can do nothing without the Lord. Our qualifications go out the window, because they don't mean anything without God.

"Yes, I am the vine, you are the branches, those who remain in me, and I in them, will produce much fruit," (John 15:5).

"It is not that we think we are qualified to do anything on our own. Our qualification comes from God," (2 Corinthians 3:5).

"And it came to pass as he went to Jerusalem, that he passed through the midst of Samaria and Galilee. And as he entered into a certain village, there met him ten men that were lepers, which stood afar off; and they lifted up their voices and said, 'Jesus, Master, have mercy on us.' And when he saw then he said unto them, 'Go show

yourselves unto the priests.' And it came to pass, that as they went, they were cleansed. And one of them, when he saw that he was healed, turned back, and with a loud voice glorified God. And fell down on his face at his feet, giving him thanks, and was a Samaritan."

"And Jesus answering, saying, 'Were there not ten cleansed? But where are the nine? They are not found that returned to give glory to God, save this stranger.' And he said unto him, 'Arise, go thy way, thy faith hath made thee whole,'" (Luke 17:11-19).

There were ten men healed but only one came back to give thanks.

He was grateful!

There were ten men healed of Leprosy, but only one came back to give thanks— and he was not of the household of faith; he was a stranger. This stranger knew that Jesus did not have to heal him. It was the mercy of the Master that showed up and allowed healing to take place. He was grateful! Remember the woman of Canaan in the 15th Chapter of Matthew? She came to Jesus asking Him to have mercy on her, but He did not speak a word to her initial request. A mother's love will produce gratitude. Her daughter was demon-possessed and she sought deliverance from the Master. *"And behold, a woman of Canaan came out of the same coasts, and cried unto him, saying, 'have mercy on me, O Lord, thou son of David, my daughter is grievously vexed with a devil.' But he answered her not a word. And his disciples came and besought him, saying 'send her away, for she cried after us,'"* (Matthew 15:22).

A heart of thanksgiving says, "You didn't have to do it, but I am so glad you did, you did this just for me." That's why we have to enter into His gates (presence) with it! What is 'it'? Thanksgiving—it is the only way to enter in. Remember that the next time you want to enter into His Presence; you have to be thankful (full of thanks) and then bless His name.

Chapter 10

HOW DO YOU KNOW YOUR PRAYERS ARE BEING HEARD

"That if thou shall confess with thy mouth the Lord Jesus, and shall believe in thine heart that God hath raised him from the dead, thou shall be saved. For with the heart man believeth unto righteousness, and with the mouth confession is made unto salvation," (Romans 10:9).

For we walk by faith not by sight. (2 Corinthians 5:7)

How does one know that they are saved? You first have to confess it with your mouth, then believe what you have just said with your heart. If you believe it in your heart, then the confession will be easy. This is an act of faith. So therefore, it is by faith that you have to believe that God hears your prayers. *"For we walk by faith not by sight,"* (2 Corinthians 5:7).This scripture has to become our testimony. We just can't walk by faith only; we must live by faith, because without faith it is impossible to please God. As we come to God, we must already believe that He hears us when we call. His word tells us so. *"Now the just shall live by faith; but if any man draw back my soul shall have no pleasure in him,"* (Hebrew 10:38).

"But without faith it is impossible to please him, for he that cometh to God must believe that he is, and that he is a rewarder of them that diligently seek him," (Hebrew 11:6).

"Wherefore, if God so clothe the grass of the field which today is, and tomorrow is cast into the oven, shall he not much more clothe you? O ye of little faith," (Matthew 6:30).

Little faith will produce little, when you go to God worrying or wondering if he is going to do it for you. We need NOW FAITH! Mark 11:24 says *"whatever things you desire, when you pray, believe that you will receive them, and you shall have them."*

Chapter 11

HINDRANCES OF PRAYER

Unanswered prayer is one of the biggest barriers to one's faith. You may have prayed for a loved one to live through an operation, but he or she died. You may have prayed for your son or daughter to stay away from drugs or out of trouble, but now they are hooked on drugs or in trouble. You may have prayed that you would not lose your job, but you did. How could a good God not answer such important requests? When God doesn't answer prayers the way we think He should, some lose the desire to follow Him, and walk away from the faith. But maybe, just maybe, there was a problem with your prayer(s), and not with God answering them. Unanswered prayer is a reality that we all need to come to grips with. Some of the greatest examples of faith did not receive a 'yes' from God.

1. *Moses led the people of Israel for 40 years, but because of his disobedience to God, he was not allowed to go into the Promised Land.*

2. *King David spent a week fasting and praying that his unborn child would not die, but his son died.*

3. *God watched Jesus, his only begotten son, suffer in the Garden of Gethsemane and heard Him call out in prayer for the cup of suffering to pass, and yet God didn't answer His prayer.*

4. *Paul prayed three times for God to remove the thorn in his flesh, God said "No, my grace is sufficient."*

When these great heroes of faith's prayers were denied, they didn't pout or turn their faith from God. So who are we to judge or critique God's character? When God doesn't answer our prayers the way we expect, know that He has a higher and greater purpose in mind. His ways are not our ways, and His thoughts are not our thoughts (Isaiah 55:8-9). God has the big picture in mind when he hears our requests.

God is outside of time, and therefore can see during and after we pray all at the same time. He is in the best position to know how to answer our requests. Keep in mind that you may be hindering your own prayers. "How?" you may ask. Here are a few examples:

· Sin Hinders Prayer

· Wrong Motives Hinders Prayer

· Lack of Faith Hinders Prayer

· God's Timing Hinders Prayer

· Insufficient Perseverance Hinders Prayer

· Not Knowing the Word Hinders Prayer

The best prayers are for God's perfect will to be done.

~

As human beings, we can often pray prayers that God will not answer—we can build barriers that hinder God from wanting to answer them. The best prayers to pray are prayers for God's perfect will to be done: not my will Lord, but Your will be done on earth as it is in heaven. Expect the Lord to move on your behalf. Do not set yourself up with preconceived ways to get your answer. Allow God to be God.

As you move forward, always remember that your Heavenly Father is always there to lead and guide you through whatever circumstances may come your way. When you pray, don't try and figure out how God is going to do it; just know that he is able, and leave the details to the Master. Most times, our troubles and problems come when we say it should have gone a certain way. We already have made up in our minds that God is going to do this or that and the other. That is a setup from the devil, your enemy, for disappointment and disbelief because you'll be looking for your answer to come a certain way. And when it doesn't come that way, you begin to believe that God didn't answer your prayer.

Ask God to give you insight through his Spirit, to

recognize how he is answering. In Isaiah 55:8-9, He tells us, *"For my thoughts are not your thoughts, nor are your ways my ways. For as the heavens are higher than the earth, so are my ways higher than your ways, and my thoughts than your thoughts."*

Let me give you a testimony here. I was counseling this couple that was going through something in their marriage. We met every week, and they could not come together to resolve this issue.

On one of our last meetings, I prayed that God our Father would intervene and restore this marriage. They came to church week one after the prayer and told me that one of their cars had broken down, so they had to ride together to and from work and do everything together in that one car. This couple complained and blamed Satan for this car being broken, when Romans 8:28 clearly says *all things work together for our good.*

The next time I saw them, the Lord had healed their marriage by putting them in the same car day after day.

God has a way of fixing things. A broken car healed this marriage. Instead of arguing, they began to pray together.

Ephesians 3:20 says *"now unto him that is able to do exceeding abundantly above all that we ask or think, according to the power that works in us."*

God bless you!

Enjoy a life full of God's blessings.

A TIME OF REFLECTION

Now after completing this book, what have you learned? How will you apply what you have learned to your prayer life? What are your prayer goals moving forward?

_____

_____

_____

_____

_____

_____

_____

_____

_____

_____

_____

_____

_____

_____

_____

_____

_____

Pastor Peggy Ratliff is an anointed and practical Biblical teacher fueled by a passion to fulfill God's mandate. She walks closely in ministry with her husband Benton Ratliff, currently serving as the Pastor of Holy Trinity Outreach Ministries in Metairie, Louisiana. Her life and testimony has helped many people find hope and restoration through Jesus Christ. A mentor and trainer of leaders, Pastor Peggy Ratliff teaches on a number of topics with a particular focus on the family, marriage, relationships, and walking in freedom. Her candid communication style allows her to share openly and practically about her experiences so others can apply what she has learned to their lives.

For more information about bulk purchases, speaking engagements, and book signings or additional products:

Please Contact Pastor Peggy Ratliff
1-866-940-3339 or
www.pastorpeggy.org

Call in for Prayer with
Pastor Peggy Ratliff
Every Tuesday Night @ 9pm CST

"Revelation Revealed"
1-857-232-0155 code 742398#

www.ingramcontent.com/pod-product-compliance
Lightning Source LLC
Chambersburg PA
CBHW032029040426
42448CB00006B/786